In the Perennial Garden

poems by

Ann Sheils

Finishing Line Press
Georgetown, Kentucky

In the Perennial Garden

Copyright © 2017 by Ann Sheils
ISBN 978-1-63534-121-8 First Edition
All rights reserved under International and Pan-American Copyright Conventions.
No part of this book may be reproduced in any manner whatsoever without written permission from the publisher, except in the case of brief quotations embodied in critical articles and reviews.

ACKNOWLEDGMENTS

The Anglican Theological Review—"Transfiguration"
Dappled Things—"The Garden"
Falling Star Magazine—"The Stream"
Gray's Sporting Journal—"From Eden"
The Wayfarer—"Trio in the San Juans"
TWJ Magazine—"Home"
TWJ Magazine Newsletter—"Francisco"

Publisher: Leah Maines

Editor: Christen Kincaid

Cover Art: license agreement from Shutterstuff

Author Photo: Kay Aiken Sheils

Cover Design: Elizabeth Maines

Printed in the USA on acid-free paper.
Order online: www.finishinglinepress.com
       also available on amazon.com

Author inquiries and mail orders:
Finishing Line Press
P. O. Box 1626
Georgetown, Kentucky 40324
U. S. A.

Table of Contents

"From Eden" 1
"The Garden" 3
"The Stream" 4
"April" 5
"Death in Christmas" 6
"Evening News" 7
"Francisco" 8
"Above St. Augustine" 9
"Confession" 10
"Pruning Myrtles" 11
"It Shall Be Devoured" 12
"In the Perennial Garden" 13
"Nag's Head" 14
"Casting" 15
"Morning Prayer Redux" 16
"Et in Arcadia Ego" 17
"Home" 19
"Transfiguration" 20
"The Letter" 21
"Trio in the San Juans" 22
"Grafting" 23
"Echoes" 24
"Nandina" 25
"Grazing the Beast" 26
"Hearth Cricket" 27
"Tribute" 28
"Solstice" 29
"Dogwoods" 30
"Lab Test" 31
"Late Storm" 32

From Eden
>   *for Mallie Exley*

In my cornstalk palisade,
armed with sunscreen, ear-plugs, and UV glasses,
I watch for ever-scarcer dove
on a foam-lined swivel seat,
replete with shells, cold drinks and snakebite kit,
though there's greater danger now from ants,
scavengers whose fiery bites and matriarchs,
whose talent for communal life,
surely will inherit them the earth.

A jeep has brought me to my station.
Hardly aerobic, this sport,
modern conscience nags.
And someone's left his truck so close
that western sun glints on the glass
like a thousand neon lights.
I wonder why I crouch in camouflage.

The birds don't fly.
The sun eases down,
degree by slow degree.
I break a long dead stalk of corn
and chew it out of boredom,
amazed that there's the slightest trace
of tender summer green,
like the whispy scent remaining
long after the press of flesh on flesh.

Why always in the woods
is there this ache of pleasure?
Does the earth thrum up some primal pulse?
Or is this a distant call
from that lost pair in the garden,

or a simple oneness with the season,
wearing the harvest on my shoulders,
matching its tawny fields and mottled remnant greens,
trading the electric hum of home
for the sibilance of cornstalks,
and a wet winter wind.
We are hunting here, to be alive,
even if no gray dove ghost down,
out of the dove-gray sky.

The Garden

He who created enmity
between the serpent's head and me,
did the job as well as only He can do.
And those insisting that a snake
is more afraid of me than I of him,
have never seen a thick king snake
unwind his long muscle
from an oak tree limb
onto my baby's swing,
despite shells and pinecones
hurled at his determined head,
nor seen a rat snake's lazy undulation
cross my two ton tractor's roaring path.

We may undo somewhat the curse of labor
with computers and machines,
find anodynes for pangs of birth and death,
but the subtlety of the serpent still prevails,
blighting our wary walks,
his head poised to startle us
in the garden cutting flowers.

The Stream

The friction of the southeast trades
urges surface water into small verticals,
while the earth's spin
seizes the slanted spray
and flings it westward,
until, disgorged from the swollen Gulf,
it pours back to the Atlantic.

Others blithely cross this jewel stream.
But above the diesels' roar
and the slash of twin propellers
through its six-knot flow,
so wide and deep
its volume equals
a thousand Mississippis,
I hear Pip's demented cry.

On this crossing
I learn about a recent castaway,
who, bound for Bimini,
fell from the gleaming fiberglass,
his screams masked by sea-slap
and the engines' throb.

Did terror come first
with the blue-sailed man-o-war,
or with the shark's insistent bumps
against his dangling legs,
helpless as an infant's?
Did he gape at starfish
in the inverted heaven
stretching endlessly beneath him?
And did he rage like Pip,
like all appalled by loneliness,
at the resolute backs
turned away?

April

is cruel,
even in a hot country
where soon we will be cloyed
by jasmine and magnolia.
Now we sleep with open windows
free from the mumble of AC,
breezes stirring sheets,
oak leaves cascading like rain.

Before dawn come the growls
of a martial mammal battling
whatever shrieks its surrender.
When darkness drains away,
I search for carcasses or blood,
but find no clue.
In another week barbarity comes again,
and at dawn no trace.
Was it mating—
futile female cries, snarls of subjugation?

Killing or conquest seeps into my spring.
I wander dazed
through budding and unfolding—
nighttime brutality bleeding on April blooms.

Death in Christmas

"Bring a gun," my husband shouts from the yard,
his voice barely audible over the barks and snarls
that announce a battle between our old terrier
and an errant raccoon from the marsh.
It's raining—indoors grown children
have reprised their Christmas custom
of baking gingerbread together.

My son sprints from the kitchen with a rifle
and reaches it into the fray—
there are hunters' tales of coons
shredding ears, scratching eyes, even drowning dogs.
But this one seems more pitiable.
Seeing frightened eyes in a masked face,
my son grieves to kill it—says it has shat itself.

Then we begin the contest with other fatality.
The dog is vaccinated, we are not,
but the Health Department's closed for Christmas,
and they lost the last cadaver that we took for testing.
So I glove and carry the soiled dog at arm's length,
in the hope that washing saliva, blood, and feces,
bleaching tub and towels,
will safeguard us from rabies,
though my gardener's hands are nicked,
my arms scratched from putting up the tree.

So death comes to Christmas,
but there have already been the small deaths—
old insults, heartaches, enmities—
that tarnish our festivity.

Evening News

Tethered to my car by suburban chores,
distracted by a radio companion,
I hear but can't absorb
news singularly new:
that in a nanosecond
matter smaller than a proton
exploded to create the universe,
imprinting space-time's fabric
with primeval wrinkles,
older than the galaxies
by at least five billion years.
A persuasive voice intones
that within a generation
we'll understand the world's creation.

Then I recall the story of a traveler
in route to interview Tibetan monks,
who had sought throughout their history
to learn and to record
all the names of God.
As the traveler approached the monastery,
climbing to its summit in the dark,
all the stars above him,
blinked out one by one.

I grip my wheel more firmly
and glance at the setting sun,
to see if it still hangs
in the west where it belongs.

Francisco

You who have nothing
except hardened hands
and a generous heart,
tend my yard
as though it were the one
you do not have.
Long after being paid,
you linger, nursing tender shoots
gleaned from cleaning beds,
preparing them
for my waiting garden.

We admire your character,
but what do you think of us?
Your improving English
might allow you to describe
the lawyers and businessmen
whose fetes and wedding parties
you clean our splendid lawns for.
Do you judge our calculated charity,
the grudging rides provided to varied housing
when your truck won't run?
I chide you for generosity—
"You can't fix the lives of everyone"—
when you send money to a deadbeat cousin
so his mother can have a child beside her
while she dies in Mexico.

For some reason
you would absolve us,
having seen worse humanity
in your rough life.
But you have seen better too,
among those who help and share and love
because it is all they have to give.

Above St. Augustine

No one photographs
the sinuous mottled forms
on the empty shore of this resort,
neglected now for Disney fabrications.
From sand emerges such a harmony
of limestone permanence
and ocean agitation
that I long to sink into its curves.

Tourists, a few miles south,
admire these stones
chiseled into famous blocks,
a military artifice.
But here, as summer afternoon
fuses into full-moon dusk,
stars blinking in small pools
of domesticated sea
caught in these recesses,
I am rapturous alone,
amid unsculpted luxury.

You should be here,
part of the voluptuous calm,
where feminine and masculine
imitate our landscape.

Confession

Tossed out of the attic,
waiting to be burned,
the box rattles
with asphalt grit and roach dung,
sags in hard winter light
that reveals yellowed notes
and rusted binders piled inside.

Burning college papers
is like burning Christmas greens.
Flames devour the brittle sheets
avidly as sappy spruce and pine,
consuming remnants of another season,
in a purge of younger themes.

Labors of a life circumscribed
by a ring of yellow light
on a long oak table;
pages of invitation
replaced by bills and tax appeals,
or surrendered in the carpool line,
where faces at the windows
signal mutely what they've lost
from within their four wheeled prisons.

Pruning Myrtles

It's only early February,
but the sun on my neck
warns that scratched and tired
though my arms may be
from probing along the bark,
feeling as much as seeing
where to let the sap flow,
I haven't much time
to outrace the swelling buds.
So I climb and lean,
risking more than I should
to pull the topmost branches
to my grasp.

Then I recall another season,
half a life ago,
when in the pleached and limber crown
of a crimson sycamore,
he risked so much
for the top-gallant brilliant leaf,
and swayed there,
framed by blue October sky,
marvelously distant,
just able to read dismay
in all our upturned faces.

He and my perfect fragile leaf
survived intact.
I was a victim of that season,
all else pruned from me but him,
like these myrtle branches sacrificed,
piled high around my ladder.

It Shall Be Devoured

The woods are down.
For three days
great clawed machines
have droned in heavy air,
mixing diesel breath
with fragrant exhalations
of broken sycamore, oak, and pine.

The ground shudders
with each fall
and men dip loud saws
into sappy wounds,
while a tractor's wide blade
scrapes the spongy forest floor
deftly as a surgeon in the womb.

Hardly a first growth canopy
over fern and needle paths—
we had cut here before.
Scrub trees and tangled underbrush
frustrated all but drunks, furtive lovers,
and cast off-dogs and cats.

We've lost primeval,
boundless and eternal.
The earth is ours
to mold with mechanical hands.
And our enlarged eyes
stretching to the stars,
see the edges of the earth,
regard the small blue seas
cupping the pied land
like fingers round a porcelain bowl.

In the Perennial Garden

> *The artists of the Renaissance...crystallized and ordered Christian symbolism...because it was the perfecting in art form of the common experience of Christian man (who)... saw God in everything.*
> George Ferguson, *Signs and Symbols in Christian Art*

Incised edges lose definition,
design undone by seasonal vicissitude,
or by the sprawl of chance-children
through careful beds
of dove-like columbine and bleeding nun;
or by the dog's delirium
in rooting out a bed of garter snakes.

Companion to toad and butterfly,
hearing the woodpecker's sharp tattoo
compete with the distant lark,
the gardener weeds and prunes,
small abortions preparing the tender earth
for the soldiering of bulbs,
until some semblance of order and succession comes,
some compromised flowering.

Nag's Head

He had,
that night in bitter January,
when snow embroidered the pale sand
and hung a veil against the void
of black Atlantic sky,
what he would later call
her white prerogative.

Earlier,
they had leaned into the keening wind,
despairing love
and disputing comfort,
which he,
from a sleek New Jersey suburb,
disdained,
but that she would never know—
whether because of gender,
or imagination,
or because her raw coastal South
hid cottonmouths beneath the garden hose,
and spun mayhem each September
out of the ocean at her door.

She saw, even then,
despite his solitary pose,
how well he fit the world,
and was not surprised
some decades later,
by his face on the highway billboard,
lover turned politico.

Casting

The day is still,
the river featureless
as the gray flat heaven it reflects.
A bateau drifts.
The shrimper spins his net across the water,
lets it sink, then tucks it with an expert wrist.

He tugs it to him,
filaments teeming with translucent shrimp,
muddy toadfish, tangled crabs—
the harvest of a fragile net
at the rich margin of the river,
once he breaks its opaque surface.

Beneath his plywood hull
the depths conceal
the almost unimagined:
winged rays, cruising hammerheads,
and, surfacing from the dark bottom,
regarding him with ancient quiet eyes,
the almost vanquished turtle,
broad backed as his bateau.

Morning Prayer Redux

The nimble goats are sheep,
and the thick slow sheep are goats
on this asphalt ribbon *Pilgrim's Progress*,
whose end is no Celestial City,
but a thin body and lean heart.
Why fear the devil's torments
or the seven deadly sins,
when cancer lurks in fatty cells,
and nearby sirens herald sudden death?

The lake that was a borrow pit
becomes bucolic:
on sapphire water, beneath a willow tree,
milk-white ducks trail their argent wedge;
a snake hieroglyphs among the cattails.
Even a nearby cardboard cut-out spire
rises whitely over the heavy trees.

Everyman is here,
but mostly Everywoman:
the gregarious in a noisy gaggle,
waddling their slow progress;
a stately solitary,
keening out "Sweet Jesus";
young mothers,
burdened in the belly or the hip;
and the angels,
ghosting by on rubber wheels,
in an almost silent rush of wind,
chiseled calves and thighs
proclaiming their salvation.

Et in Arcadia Ego

I

About suffering,
they were *sometimes* wrong, the Old Masters.
And though, after coming upon the carnage,
my dog, like Auden's, went on with his doggy life,
and we, after the cyclist died in my husband's arms,
journeyed to our destination,
I would never round that curve again
without the image of the Harley overturned.

Afterwards even weather
acknowledged this victim
more than it did Icarus.
We hiked in sun and storm,
a chiaroscuro afternoon
suddenly darkening vivid mountains
and eclipsing neon flowers.

II

After the creek's last turn
we entered the bright river.
Snugged against golden marsh,
playing in yellow light,
our boards had glided along black mud,
sheltered from autumn wind
and the scene we glided onto.

Search boats scanned the river
for the man just drowned.
On our thin boards, we inspected the shallows,
while neighbors peered under docks
and in the beds of oysters for some sign—
an empty sleeve, a boot, or a disturbance under water.

He would not be found—
the waters plied all winter
by marine patrol,
our river and our former sport
both haunted by what might be spied
in an embrace of grass or a cloak of mud.

Home

Another mother's son,
briefly in my trust,
gazes at me with eyes blue and vacant
as this empty April sky,
cloudless for months
from a fifty-year drought.

At our driveway, he is happy for a moment.
  "I know where I am. I'm at Uncle John's."
"Big Tom," I say, "how old are you?"
  "Why, almost ninety-three."
"How many men your age
have uncles who are still alive?
We are at your son's home,
where he and I have lived for over thirty years."

Tom is unconvinced,
so I begin another afternoon
with a mind besieged by generations
as tangled as the wisteria by my window;
by a tumult in which I become suspect,
an errant secretary living with his son,
whom he nonetheless forgives
with his still gentle nature.

Home is his persistent thought.
Is he home, or going home
to his wife of almost sixty years,
more than a decade dead,
who surely waits somewhere he can't remember,
or to his parents, who may not be expecting him?
Nothing I say can satisfy
this worry or this hope.

Transfiguration

Very early,
while the mountain's sloping sides
are vague pools of conifer blue and green,
smudged like children's finger paints,
and stands of slender aspens
are cobwebbed still with mist,
its peak glisters in light so focused
it seems another landscape.

Later,
the peak's familiar silhouette,
fretted by passing clouds,
bristling with spruce,
will give a name to the horizon.
But now the summit
is light made palpable,
the created heart of things,
the always so,
made joyful and new.

The Letter

"John loves you, I think," he said,
tossing the letter
into the basket by the sink,
where she kept, confused,
domestic refuse—
tax receipts and playschool news.

"Don't be silly," she laughed,
"and besides, you're worth ten of him."
As though love were measurement—
the minute calibrations
of an imaging machine
that sees beyond the skull's bony armor,
into the folded places of the brain,

Or the accurate mapping
of a rich and fabled place,
charted well and named,
then fiercely claimed.
And she thought,
"He's right, John does."

Trio in the San Juans

Mountains rear against the glass,
gilded and benign or ragged and severe,
depending on the hour or day,
steep sentinels to Ute in summer camp,
to miners, cowboys,
and to those who gather here for song,
and alabaster arms, and gleaming wood.

Chambered against stark ice,
at the New World's jagged edge,
in old timbers brought from an older wilderness,
black flagged notations
recollect solaces and pleasures,
from an age we scarcely can recall,
of wigs and whalebone, minuets in gilded rooms,
defenses, at this frontier's end, as before,
against war and loss, time and certain death.

Grafting

Now that my back
hurts while pulling weeds,
I remember my grandfather,
splaying his legs to stoop as low
as old bones would allow,
digging out the roots with patient fingers,
cleaning around his prized camellias.

He had boxes of cuttings in sand,
and seedlings, slow to burst their rock hard shell,
unpredictable in bloom, but watched for promise.
He'd tour me through his grafting beds,
gently pulling from a jar the Spanish moss
that filtered Southern sun.

I'd peer inside at the strong trunk cleanly split,
at the tender shoot uncurling its pale green flag,
learning from this green miracle,
the need to graft a lively scion
on a worn and blighted heart.

Echoes

I

Pink suffuses faded grass
this autumn afternoon.
Where there should be
brittle browns and gold,
are sasanquas' tender petals
that would reflect rosily
on a Renoir girl,
and trick us into ardent spring
in a diminished season.

II

On a mild mountain morning,
naked willow twigs
along the San Miguel
are daubed with velvet snow.
For a moment I am home
in cotton fields,
ready to be picked.

III

Raking rotted leaves
in dank August,
I see flows
of immaculate white
fallen from the myrtle,
which drift along the grass,
virginal as new snow.

Nandina

Presto, chang-o,
a large hardy nandina
shoulders it way
past stunted camellias
and blighted azaleas.
Only months ago it wasn't here.
Now abundant red berries
gleam in autumn sun.

It and scattered kin,
deadly to some creatures—
despite the name, "heavenly bamboo"—
have sprung from excrement of birds,
to flourish in cherished beds.

A hat-waving magician
has slipped it here,
where everything in this oak's understory
fights for water and my care.

Grazing the Beast

While my daughter gathers implements—
stainless pullers, picks, and combs
resembling instruments of torture—
I lead the beast whose steel misstep
could make me monopod.

Who holds whom
depends upon my anchoring
a thousand pounds of runaway,
should he so choose.
But happily the peanut brain
in its enormous bony case
is frantic over grass.

At length his snorts and breathing quiet me,
as he steams in the evening air.
I lean against the warm slab of side,
beginning to admire his coy details:
delicate lashes, velvet lips,
the nostrils' tender pink,
then succumb to the horse's charms.

Hearth Cricket

Cleaning for a party,
I spot the bronze hearth cricket
given for my marriage, many decades past,
by the freshman roommate chosen for me,
through occult wisdom of college bureaucracy.

Were we paired as opposites?
She, petite and soft,
voluptuous and kind;
I, angles and long bones—
even my new boyfriend said I was austere.

She embraced the sixties,
wrapped herself in paisley scarves,
overhung by waist-long Irish hair;
I wore jeans and college tees, boat shoes,
had pleated dresses packed away.

We lost touch, briefly re-established
by weddings, children, then divorce.
Lately, we are rejoined by writing verse,
and the twinship, glimpsed by the housing office,
has emerged at last.

How prescient the hearth cricket's contradictions,
she—loving folklore, the occult—might have known.
Did her gift allude to sweet legends of family luck and bliss,
or to earlier ones, where the cricket sings for death?

Or perhaps he sings for life and death—
for love and love lost,
by the gentle spirit who deserved it most,
for what survives and resurfaces,
like the bronze emblem clinging to my desk.

Tribute

But for you, hard January,
I could be daughterless.
You are the dense counter
to the hex and pulse of fecund April.

Outside my window, a tree of yours
thrusts its naked branches
through tender flakes, toward heaven,
though rooted in ice to once soft earth.

This same tree I watched all that winter day,
from strong noon to the slant light of evening,
regarding from my bed the scarred burls
which mimicked my veined and rounded belly,

until it was time to claim
her, who from the spinning
of more than half the seasons,
came to me,
from yielding spring into iron winter.

Solstice

How to have known—
with trees heavy-maned,
tossing warm sounds
to the bed where we lay,
notched and fitted
like new, smooth lumber,
sticky with sap and pungent—
that the year had begun its slow subside
into the slanted light of the other equinox,
and that passion had begun unraveling
its frail and iron thread.

Long years later I climb the stairs,
no longer two-by-two,
tired and tarnished as all lovers become,
to that room where we,
charmed exceptions,
recovered halves of ourselves,
had even breathed together.
Nothing unblemished remains
from that distant season.
Only bones lie cleanly
under freighted flesh and a scarred heart,
both burdened by births and deaths
and corrupted caring.

I mount the stairs to learn
that even when poised
on that high moment of laughing summer,
our finite hearts had bound us to a finite world,
and we were in the shadow of turning.

Dogwoods

Though she had lived a few years more
than Housman's score,
when she decided to
embroider her woods with white,
the attempt was fraught and failed
as other early plans,
doomed by drought, blight, and lassitude,
so that in this distant spring,
only a tree or two
startles her with high clean blooms,
flags unfurled
against chilled and barely budding leaves,
small white flames
burning for what she did,
and what she did not do.

Lab Test

The nurse bangs out the door—
here, exits and entrances are
inscrutable and frequent as British farce—
leaving three purple vials on the counter
(uncanny reminders of Beaujolais,
cabernet, or heavy syrah),
to be scrutinized more carefully
than the finest vintage,
measuring, instead of aldehydes or acetobates,
creatinine and leukolytes.

From the warm earth,
a winemaker extracts the grapes' goodness,
their output brilliant or closed, finished or green.
My decades have distilled a wine
waiting here to be examined
for excess and deficiency;
ready for the discovery
of what I have chosen for my essence,
yet enigmatic as to whether
I have wafted an angel's share.

Late Storm

Wind soughs in the boughs of oaks.
Another night storm rises
and tosses in tree limbs
like a restless child
who at last begins to wail.
Tomorrow it will summon him
to drag broken branches to the fire,
rake brittle palm fronds,
and lift sodden lumps
of grey moss, like carrion,
off the drive.

Restless under the burdened moon,
he arises to survey the damage,
surprised the acres are unscathed.
Other storms this winter
have torn rotten wood away,
stripped palmettos clean.

This is old age,
thick oaks pared by wind.
Disappointments have already
littered the lawn below,
and losses left their tracings in the grass.

It is not surprising that **Ann Sheils** chose a gardening theme for her recent chapbook, *In the Perennial Garden*. She has spent the last 41 years caring for land alongside her much loved Vernon River in Savannah. Few flowers have her attention. Instead she writes of snakes, storms, killing raccoons—and emblematic gardening failures.

Ann's family has been native to Savannah since its founding, though she has become a part time resident of Telluride, Colorado, where she finds inspiration from wilderness and mountains.

Ann is a graduate of Duke University, a former teacher and current realtor. She has been married for 41 years, and has three adult children. Some poems resonate with words from *The Book of Common Prayer*, and from her experience at St. Johns' Parish Church for 35 years.

She has published poems and short stories in many periodicals, including *The Anglican Theological Review, Dappled Things, The Wayfarer, Gray's Sporting Journal, Time of Singing, TJM Journal, The Aurorean*, and others. Ann has participated in writers' conferences at Sewanee, Aspen, and Ossabaw Island.

www.ingramcontent.com/pod-product-compliance
Lightning Source LLC
LaVergne TN
LVHW041601070426
835507LV00011B/1241